Thank you for picking up this coloring book.
Be on the lookout for a series of coloring books with different themes by me.

I would love to see your colored pages of my coloring books.
Please share them on Instagram, Twitter, Facebook or YouTube.
Hashtag #Drawtensil and tag me @Drawtensil
on Instagram for a chance to win a mystery prize pack.

Enjoy!
- Drawtensil

@ Copyright 2018 Drawtensil, David Lau. All rights reserved.
With the exception of artwork used for review purposes,
none of the contents of this publication may be reprinted, reproduced or distributed
in any form without the written permission of the copyright owner.

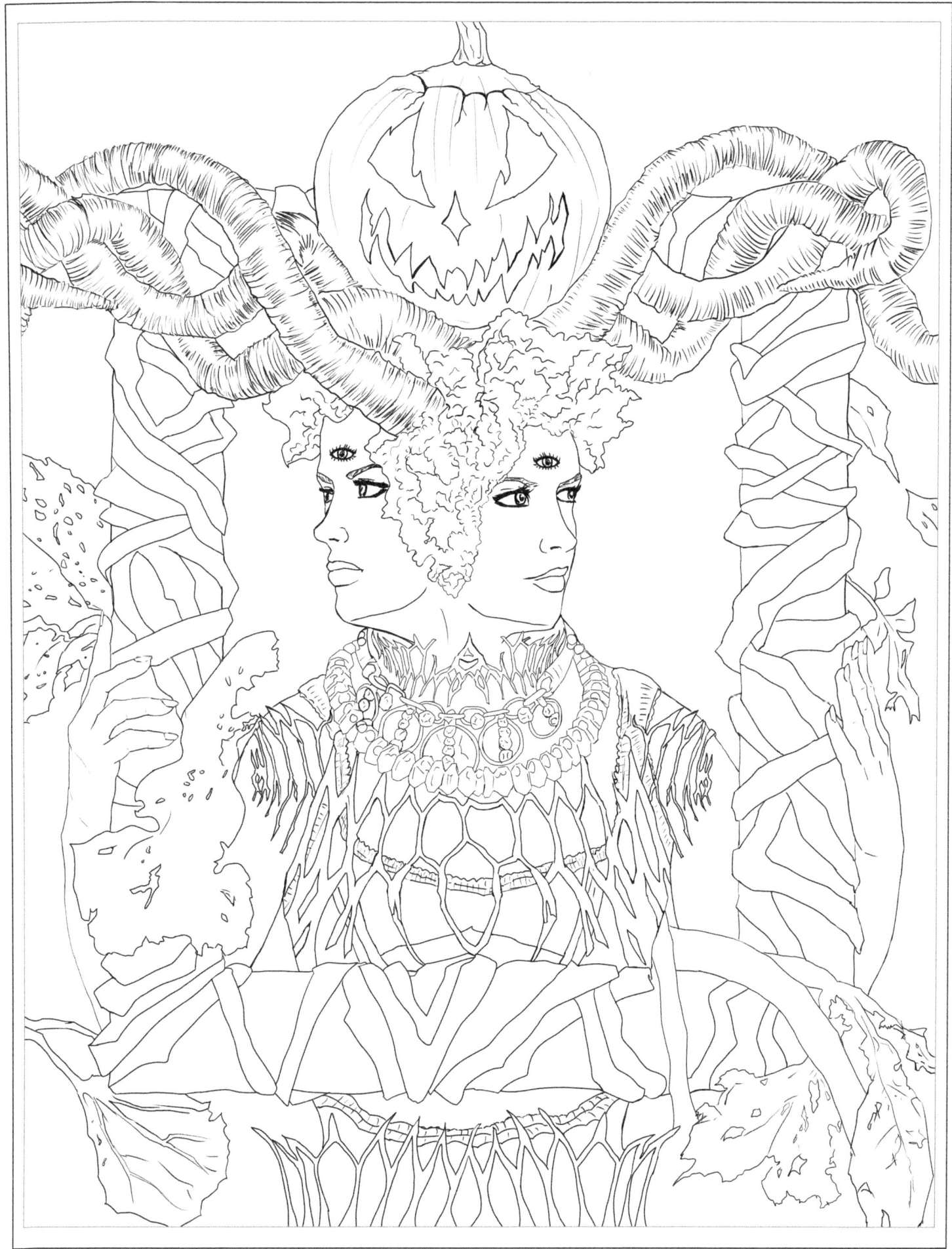

Beautiful Horror

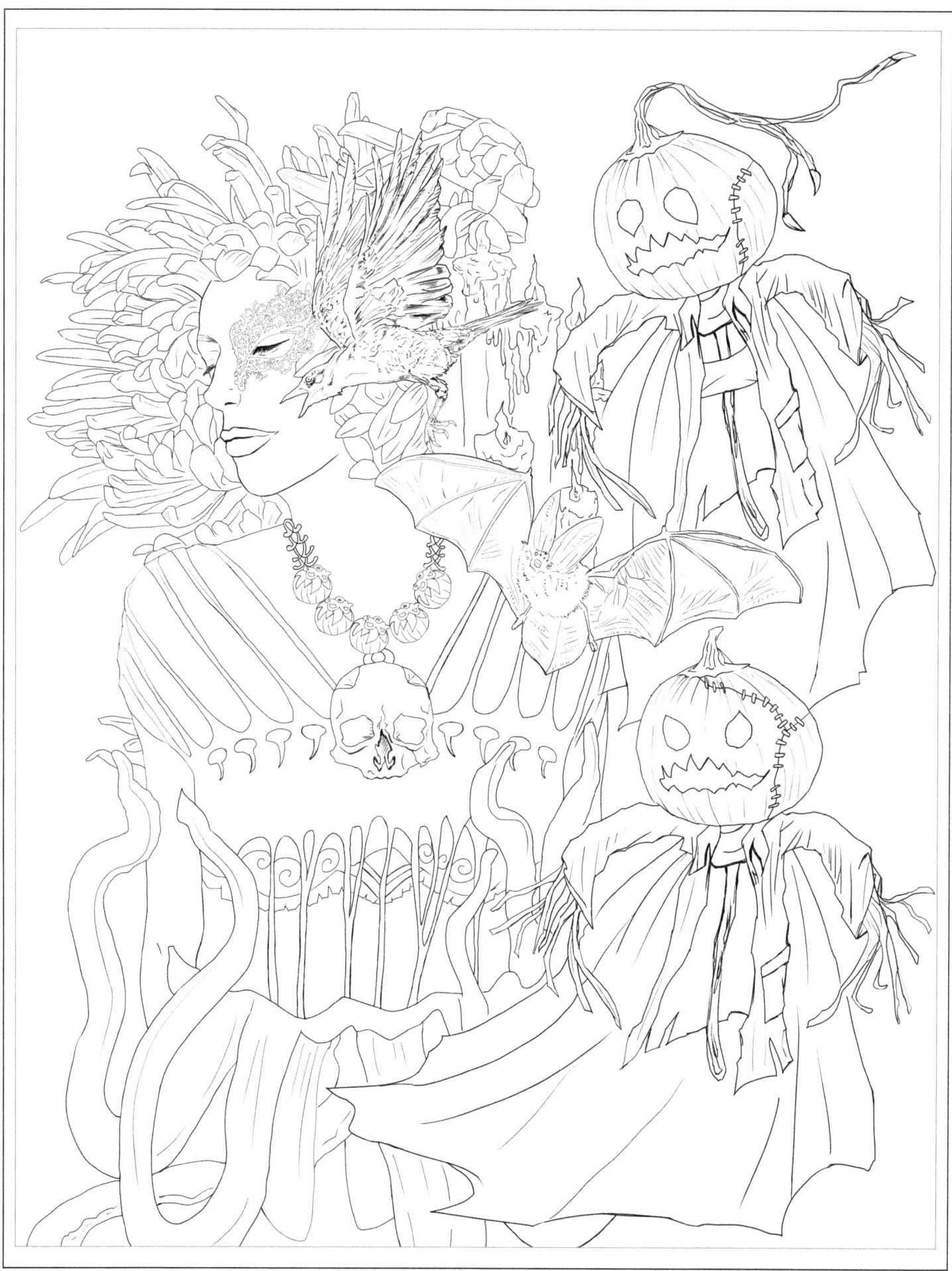

Beautiful Horror
COLORING BOOK

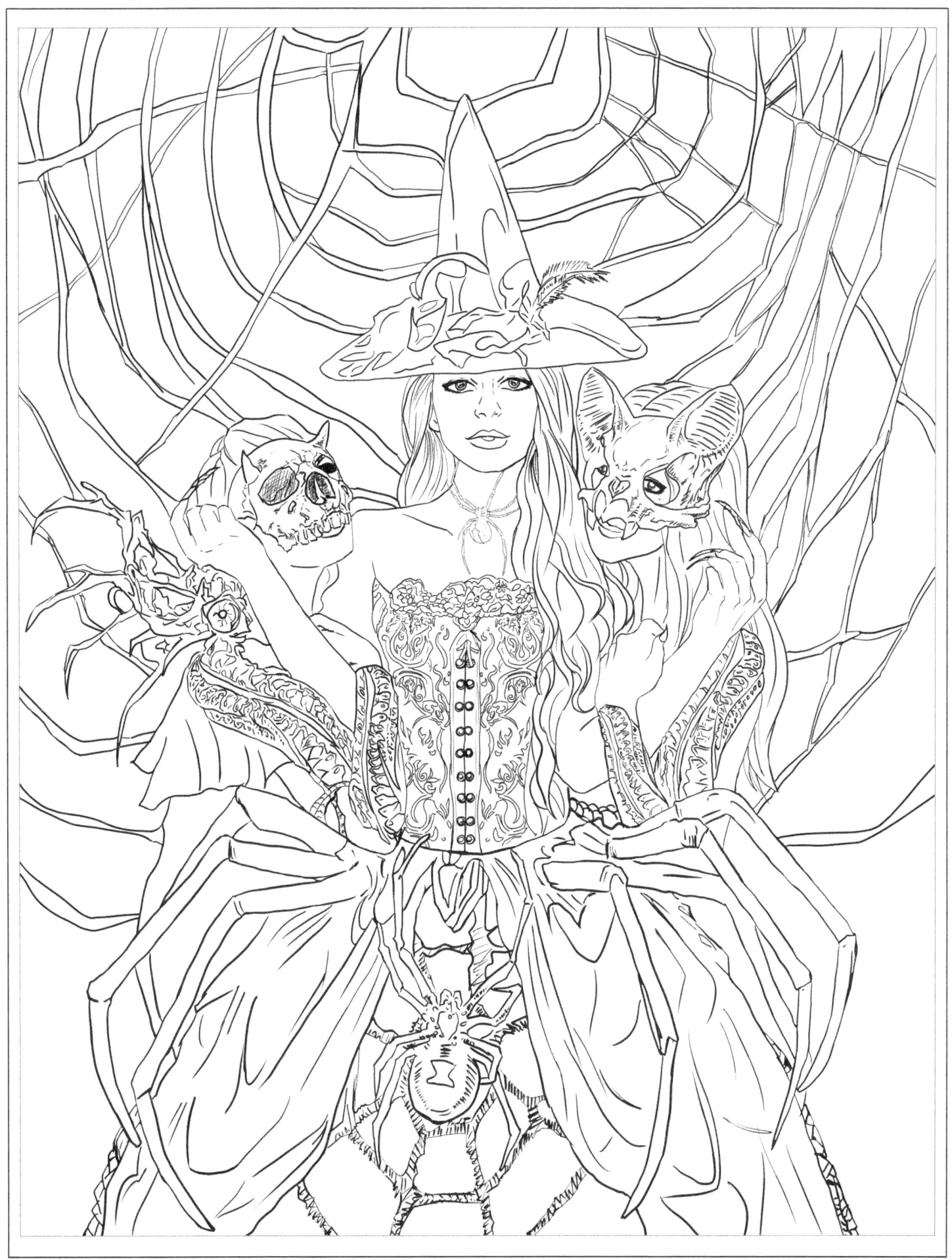

Beautiful Horror
COLORING BOOK

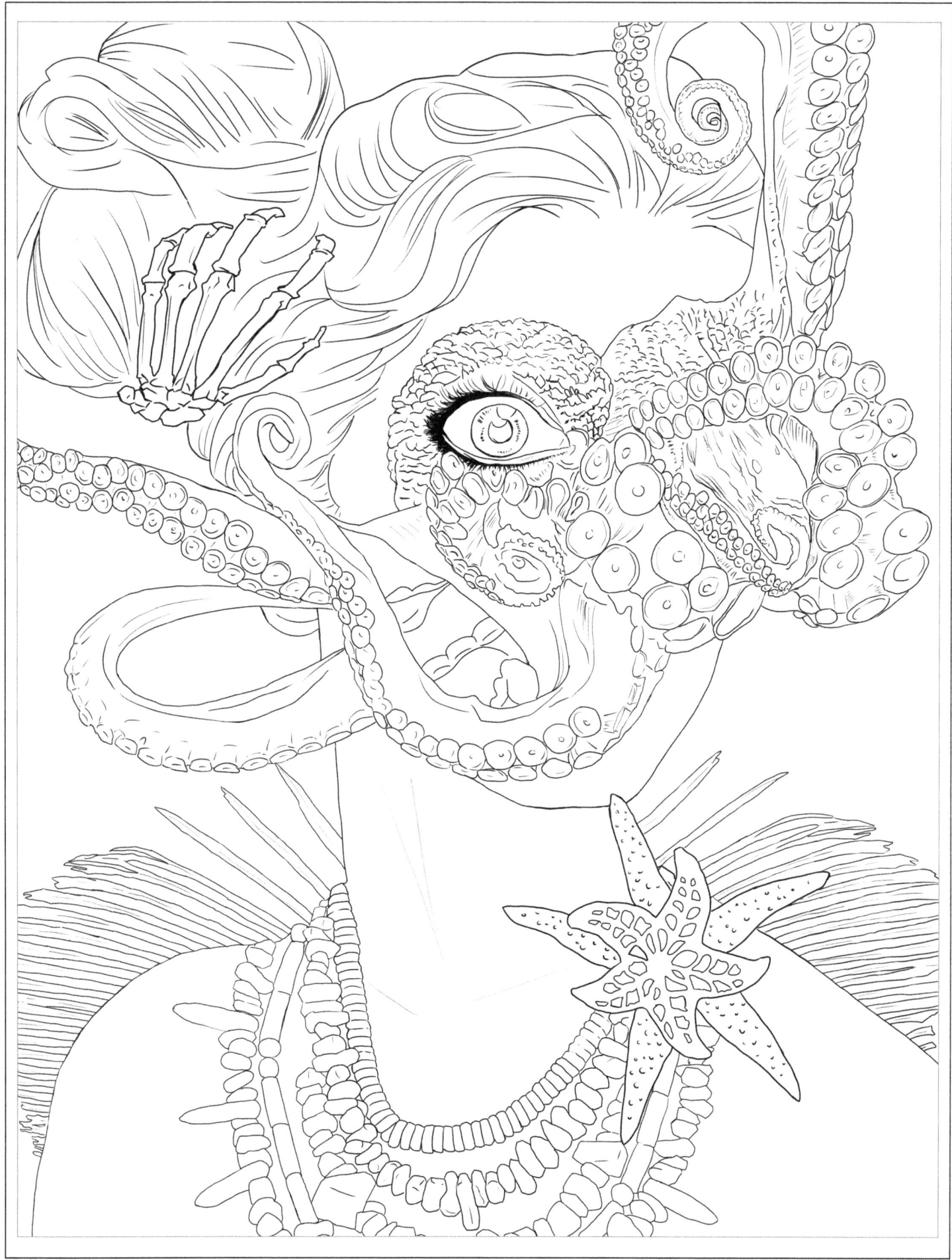

Beautiful Horror
COLORING BOOK

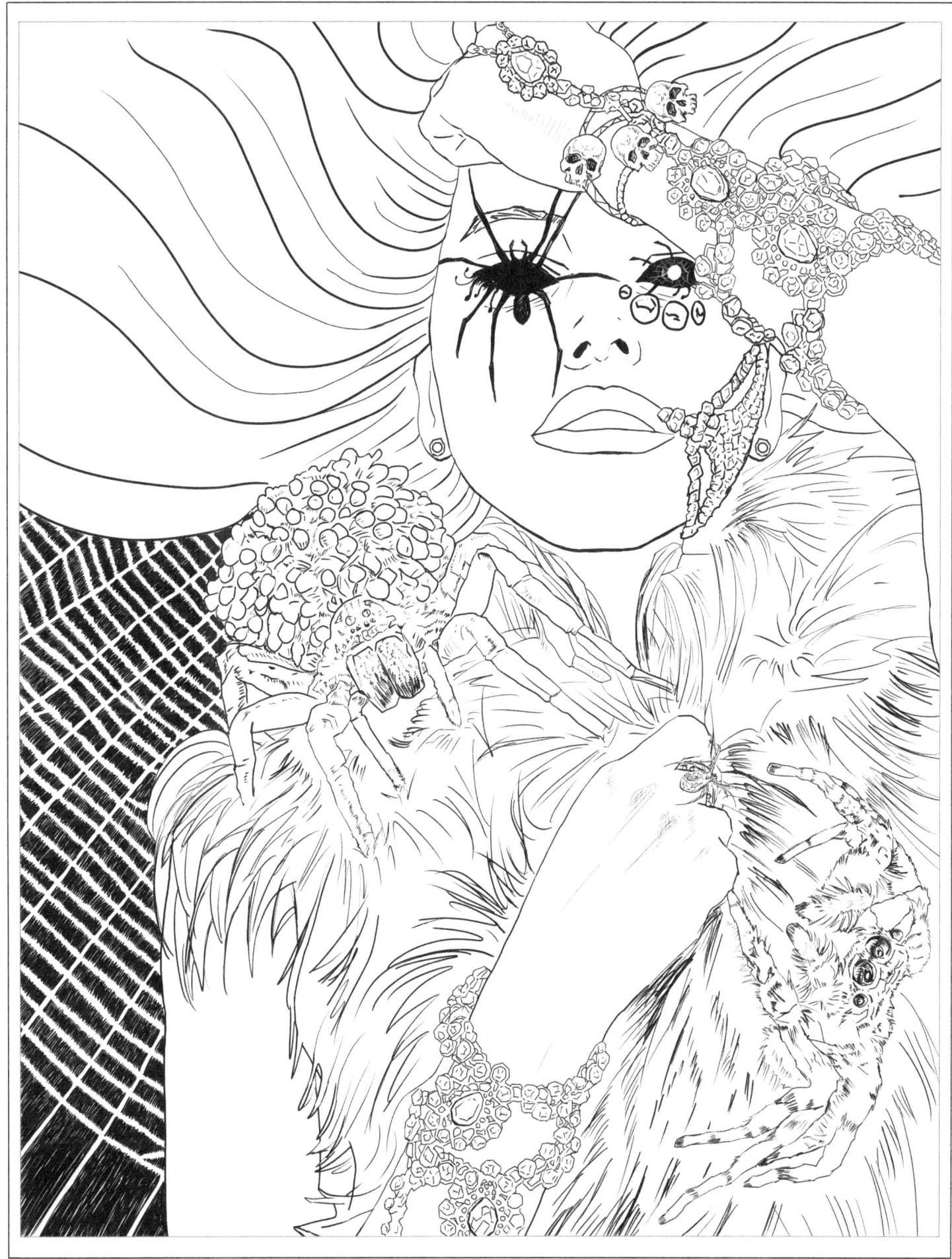

Beautiful Horror
COLORING BOOK

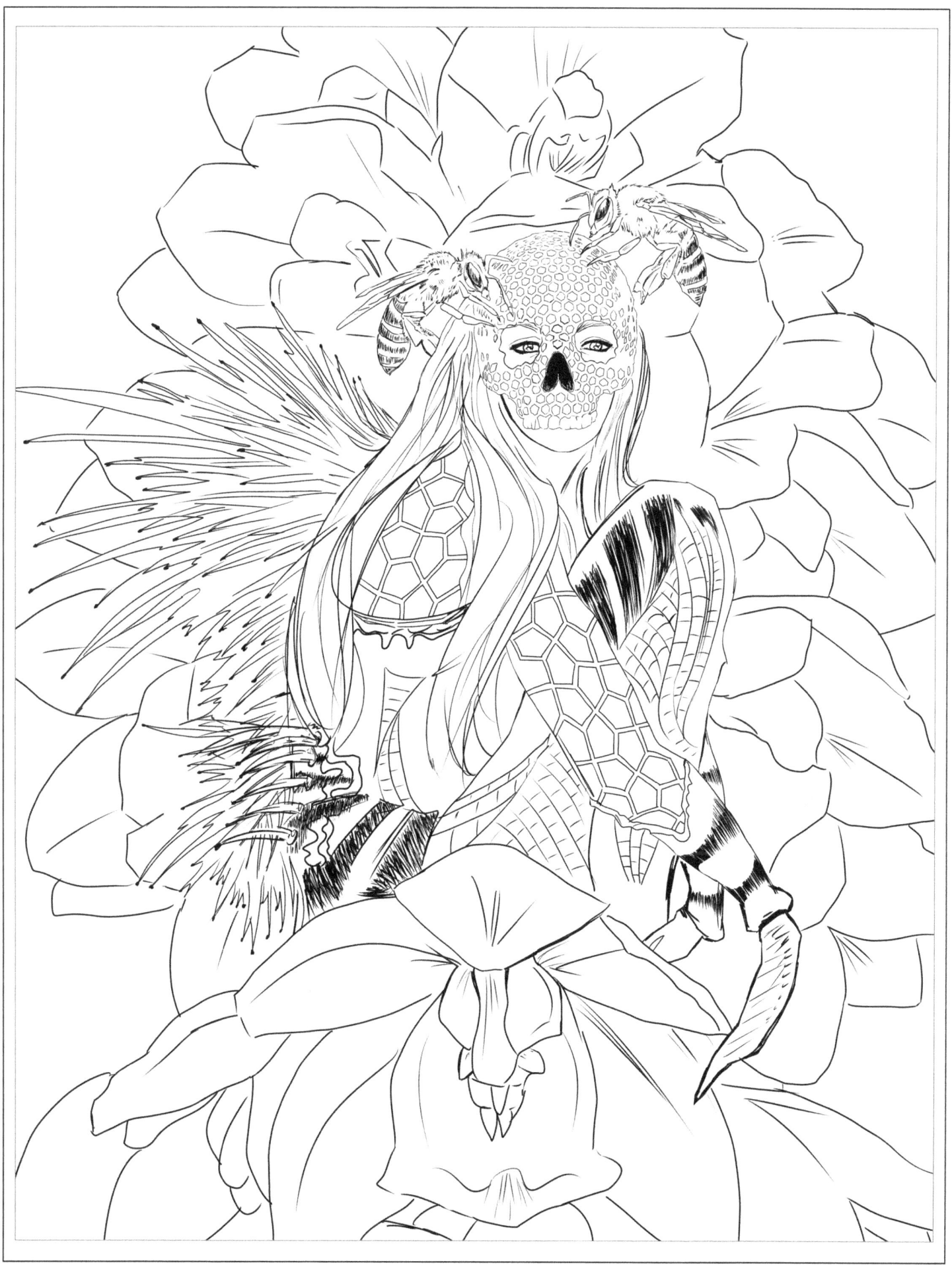

Beautiful Horror
COLORING BOOK

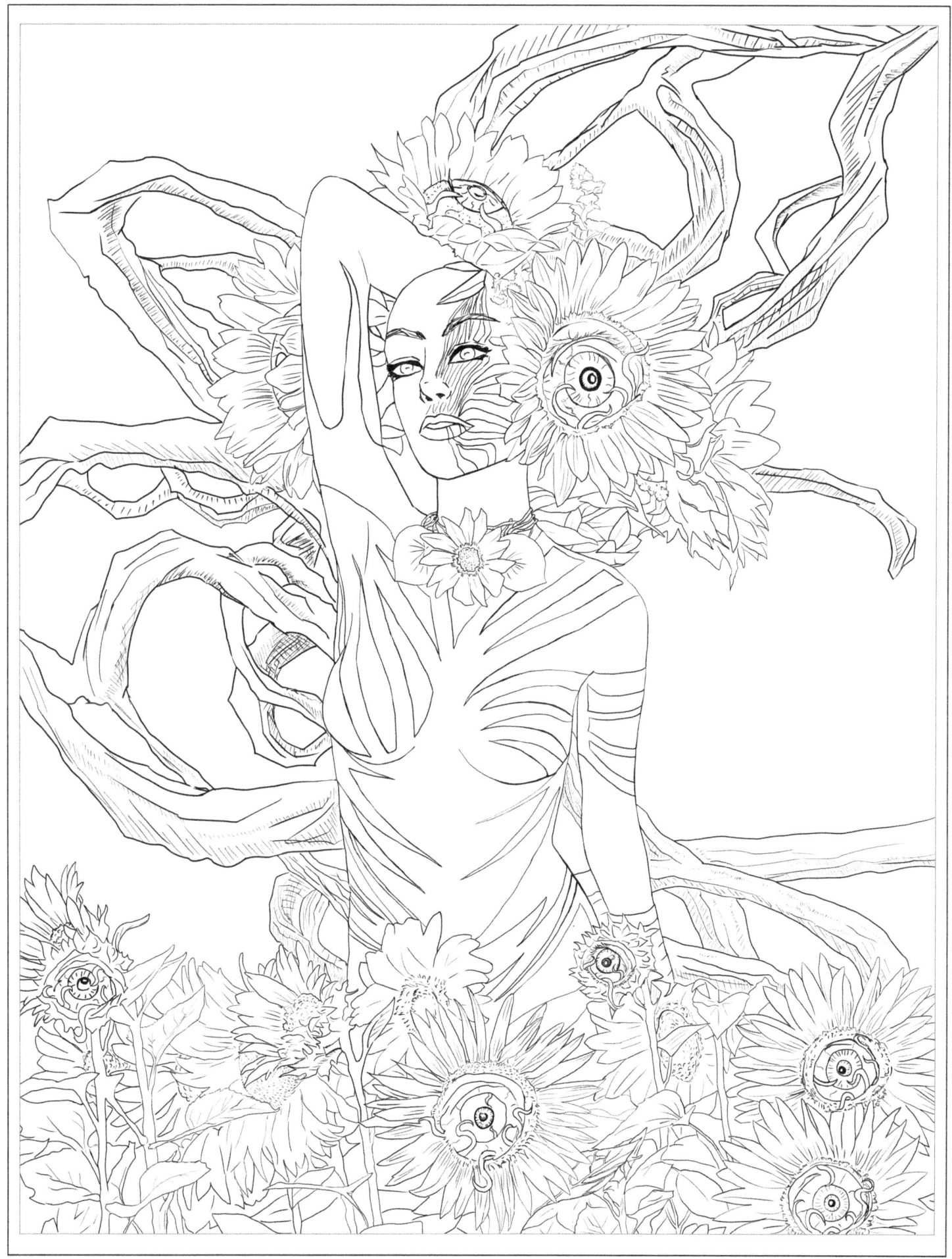

Beautiful Horror

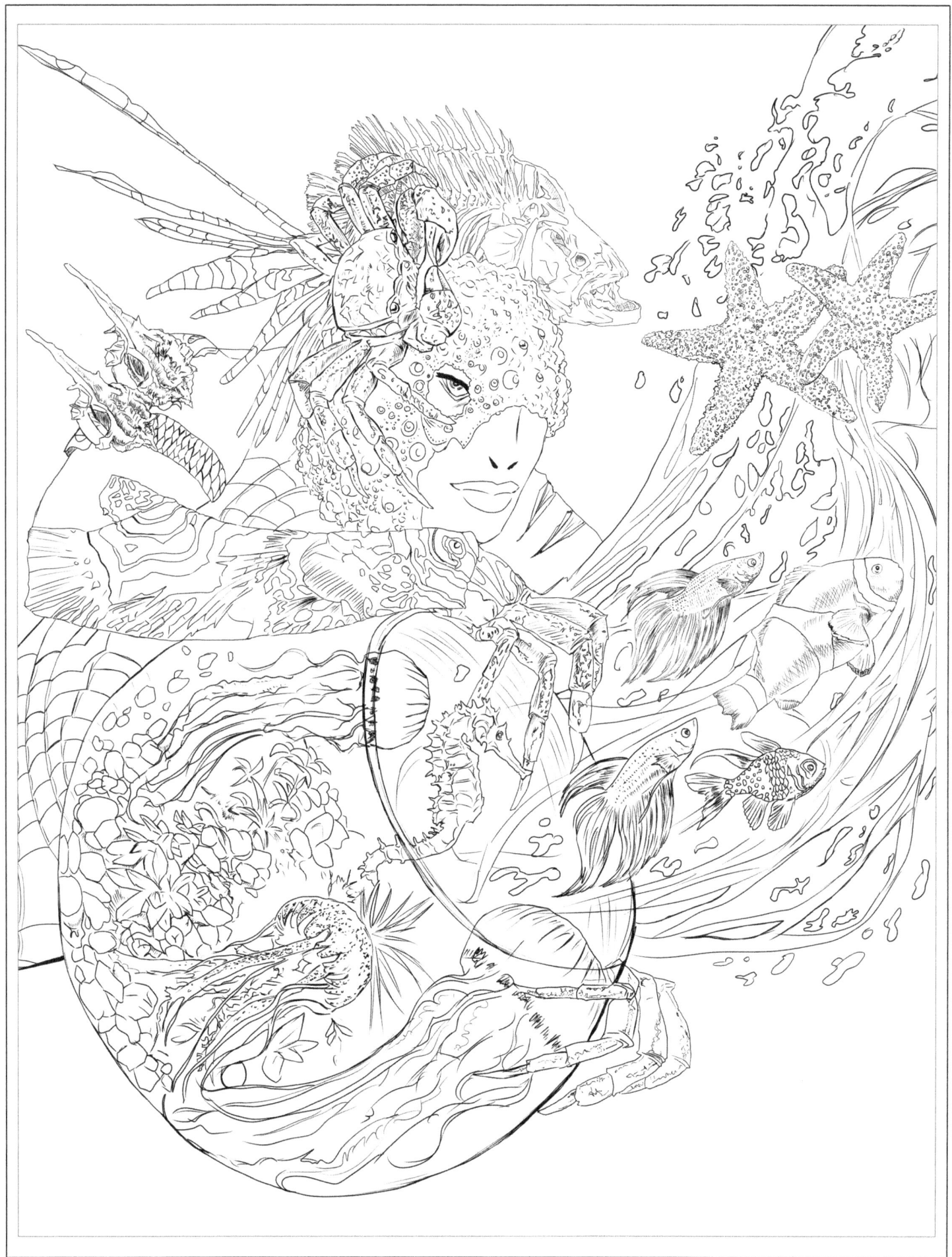

Beautiful Horror
COLORING BOOK

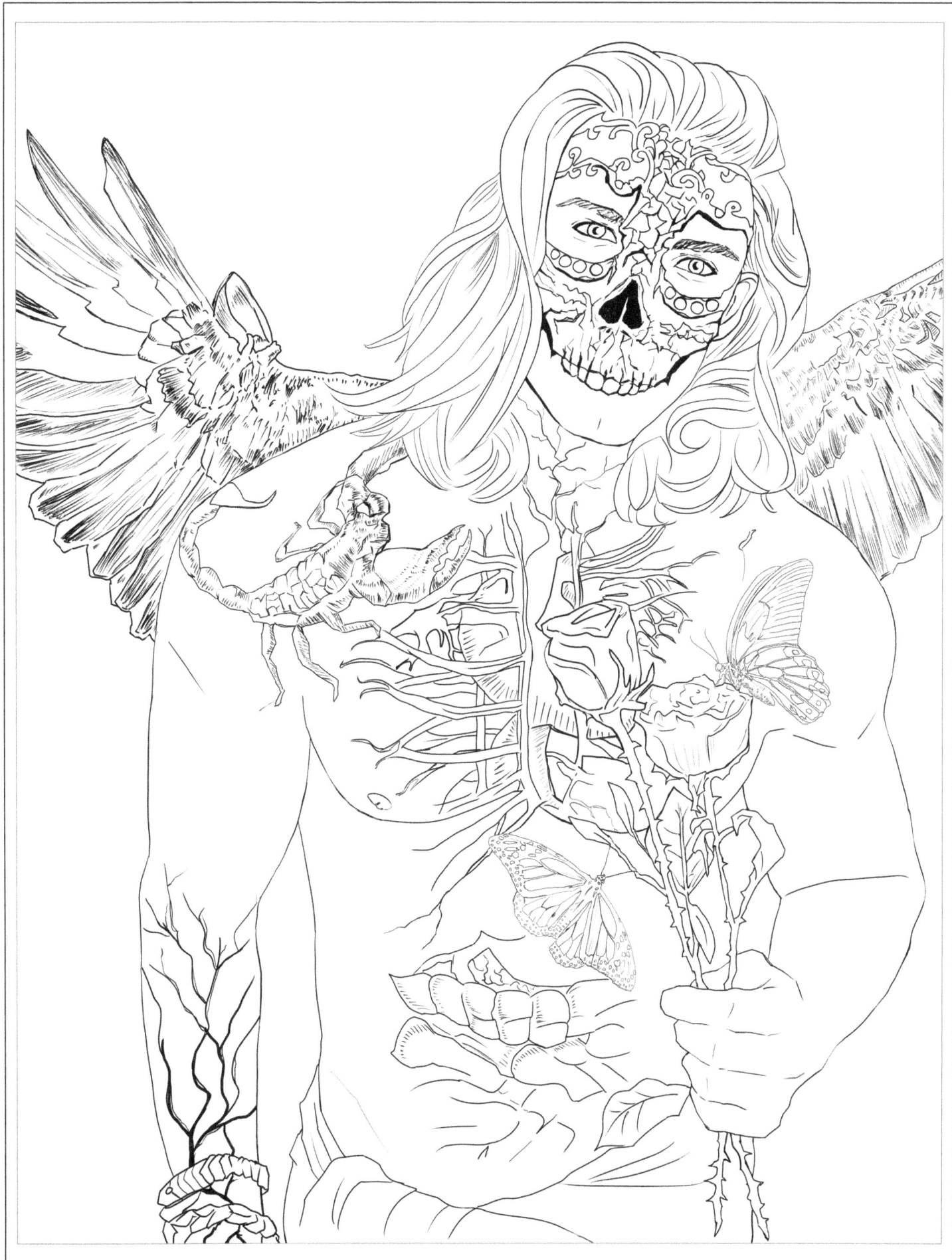

Beautiful Horror
COLORING BOOK

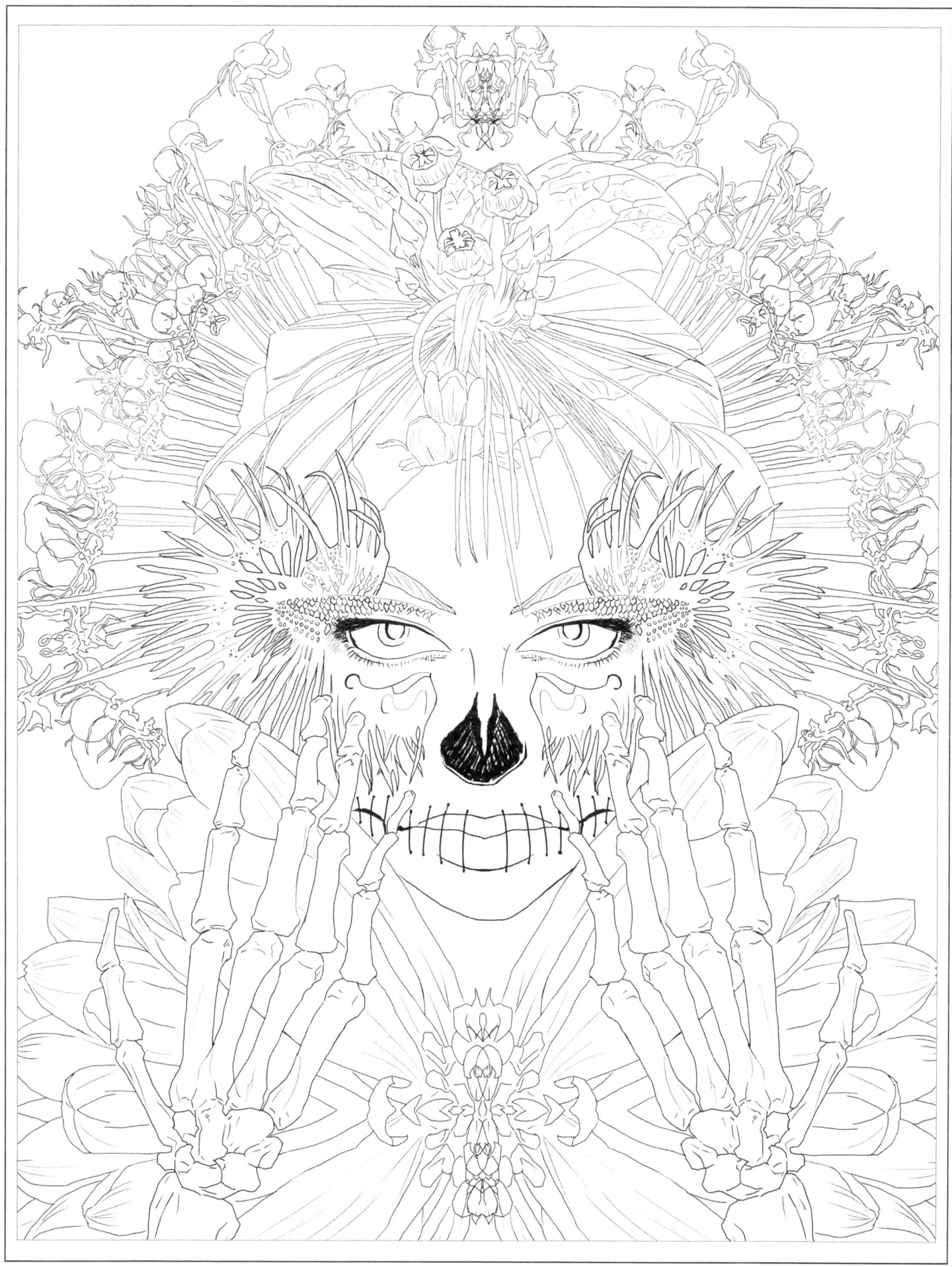

Beautiful Horror
COLOURING BOOK

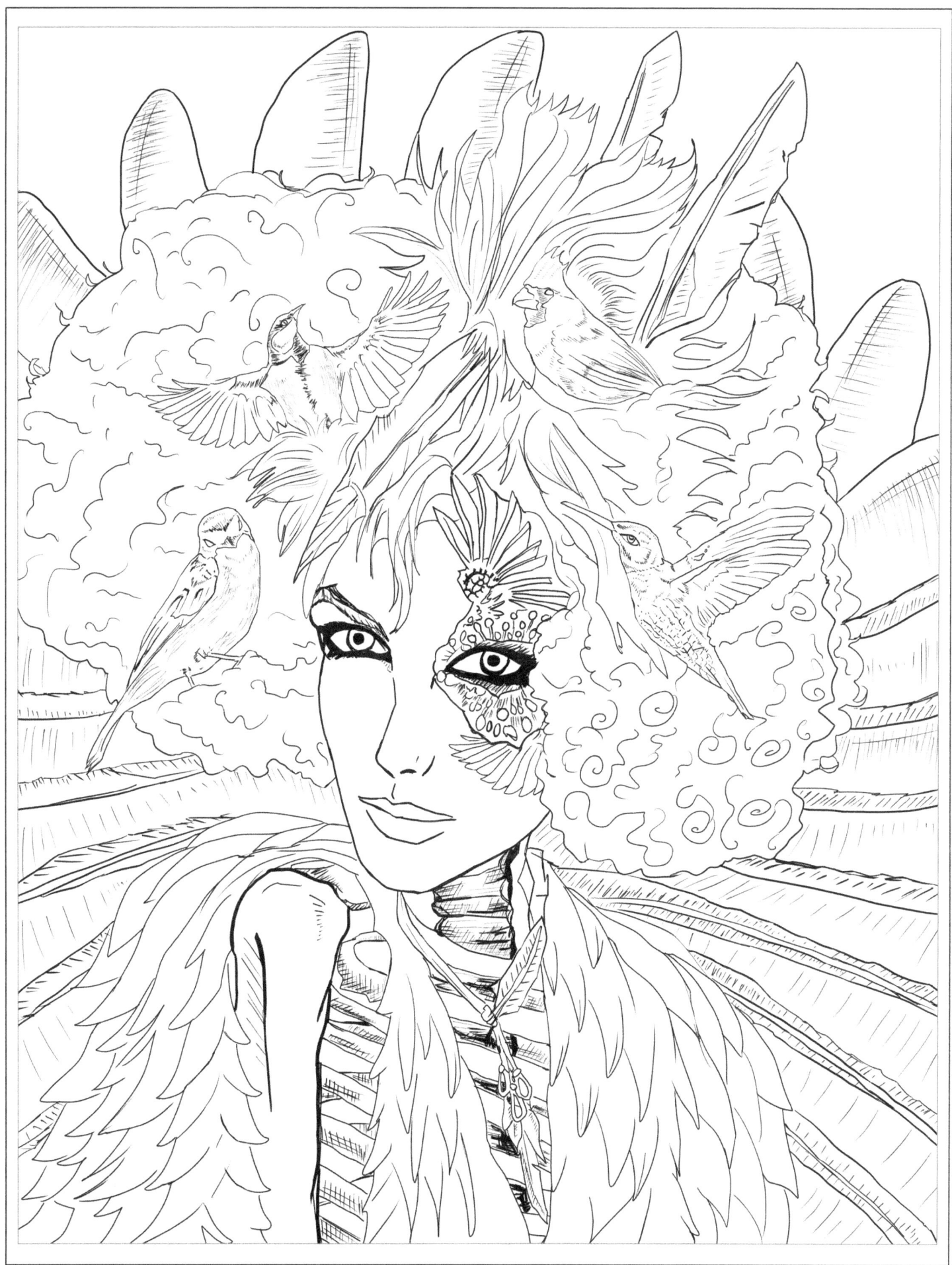

Beautiful Horror

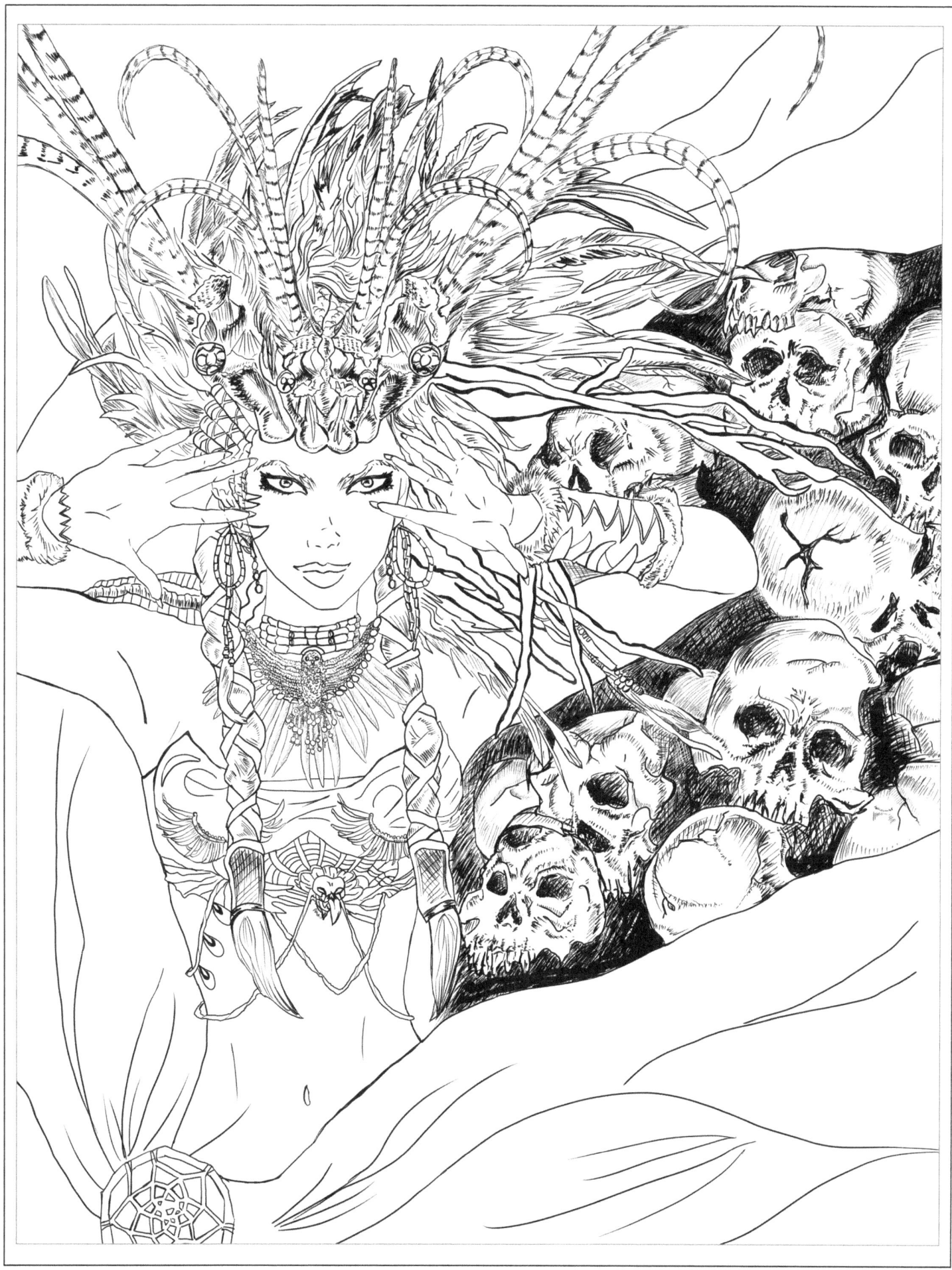

Beautiful Horror
COLORING BOOK

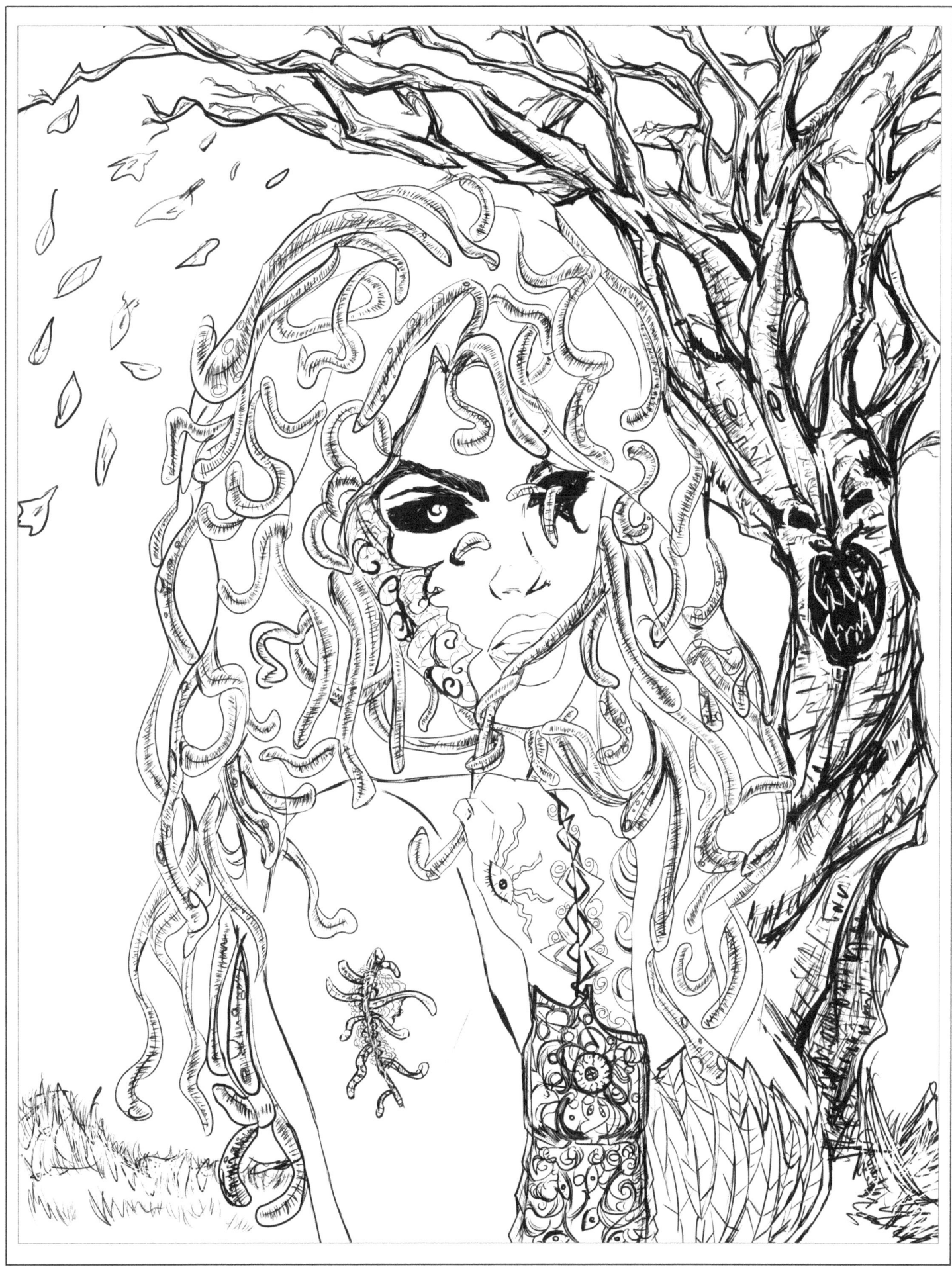

Beautiful Horror
COLORING BOOK

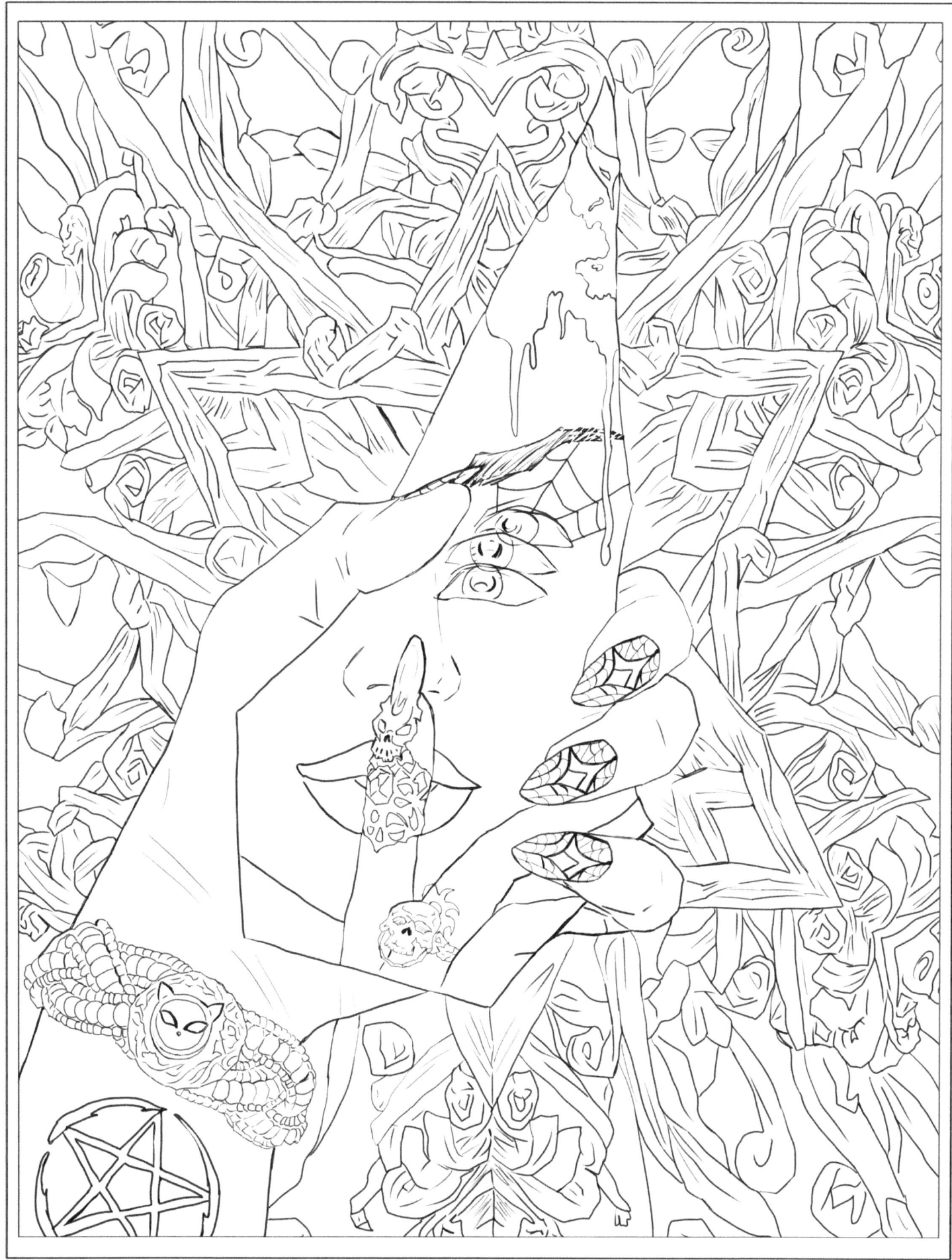

Beautiful Horror
COLORING BOOK

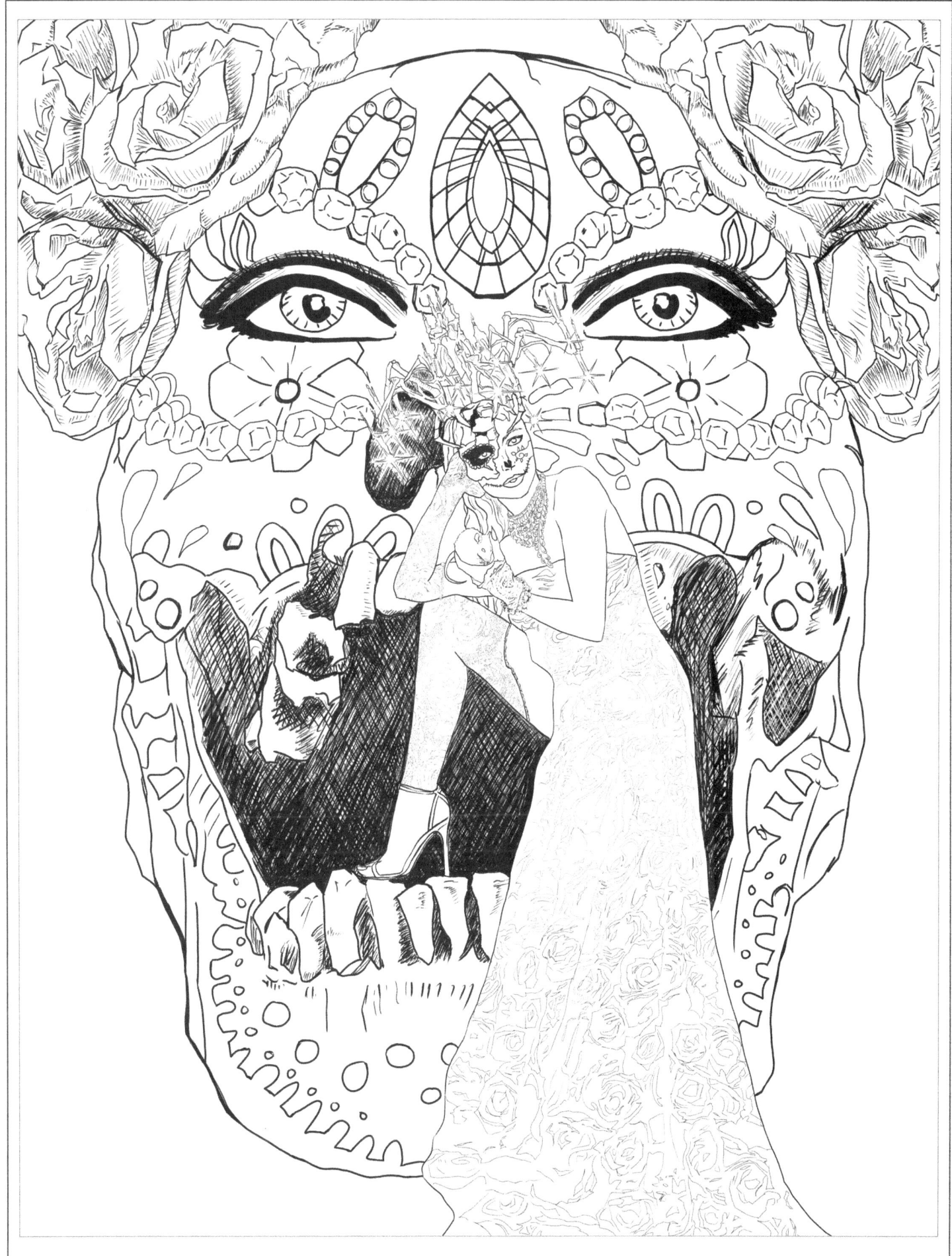

Beautiful Horror
COLORING BOOK

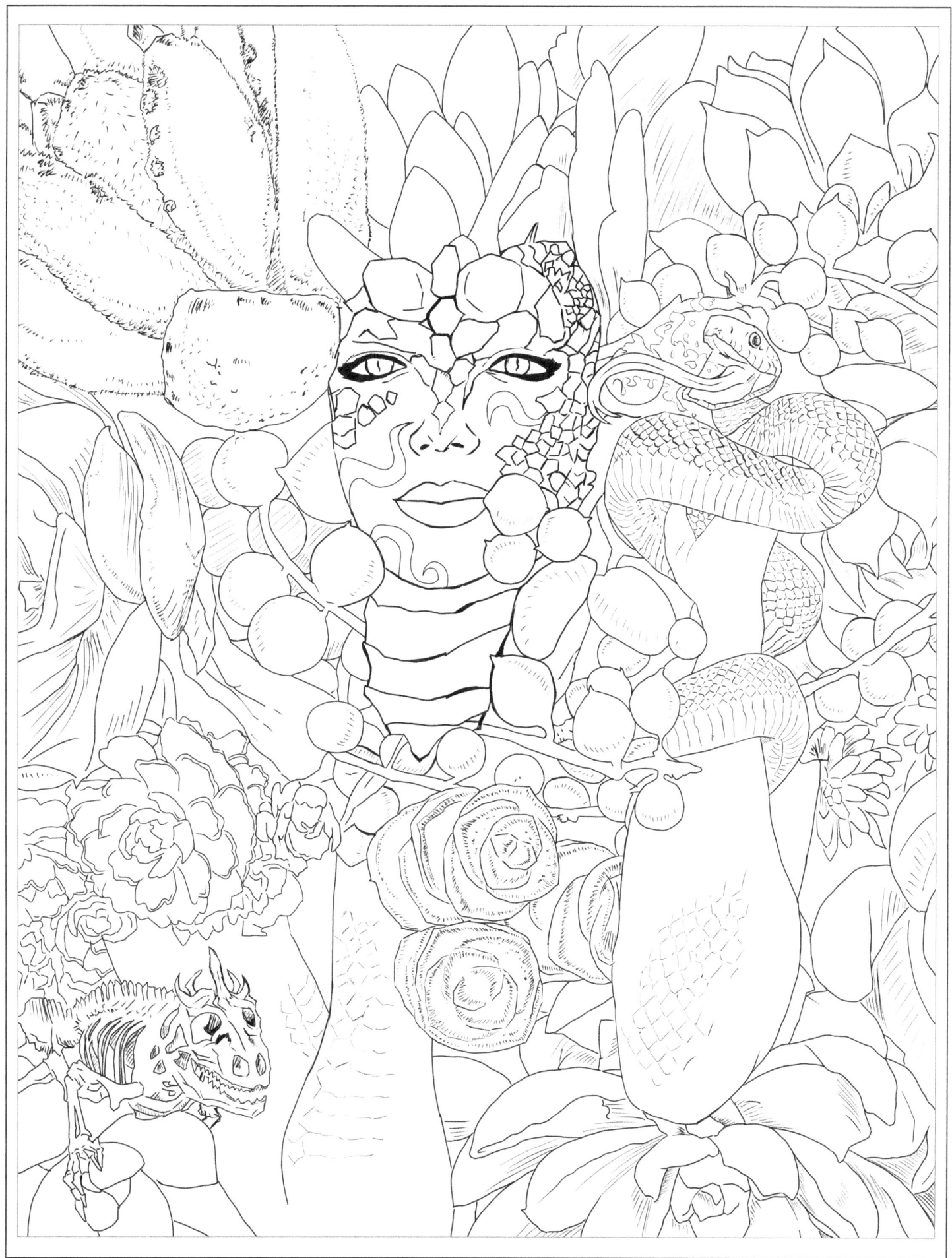

Beautiful Horror
COLORING BOOK

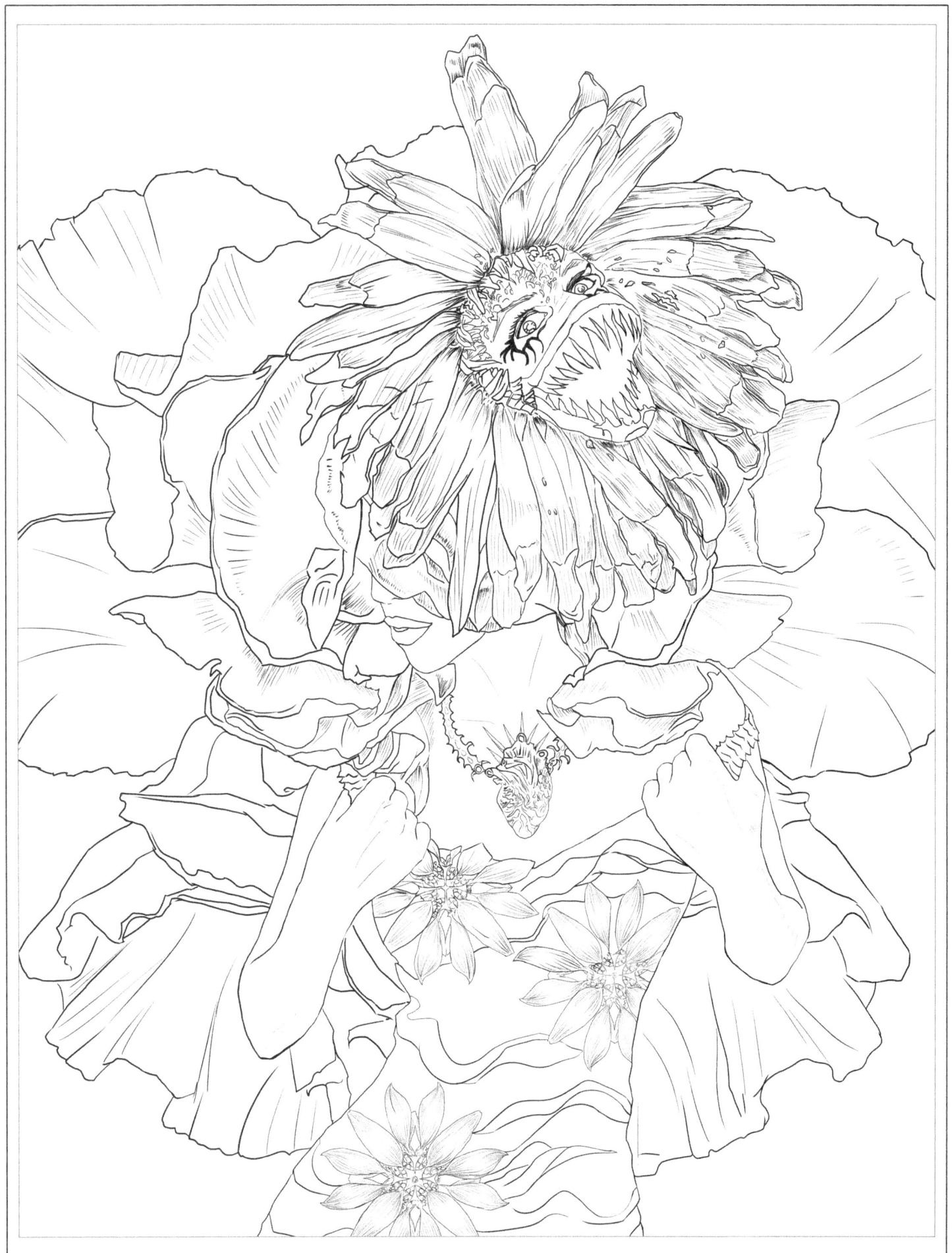

Beautiful Horror

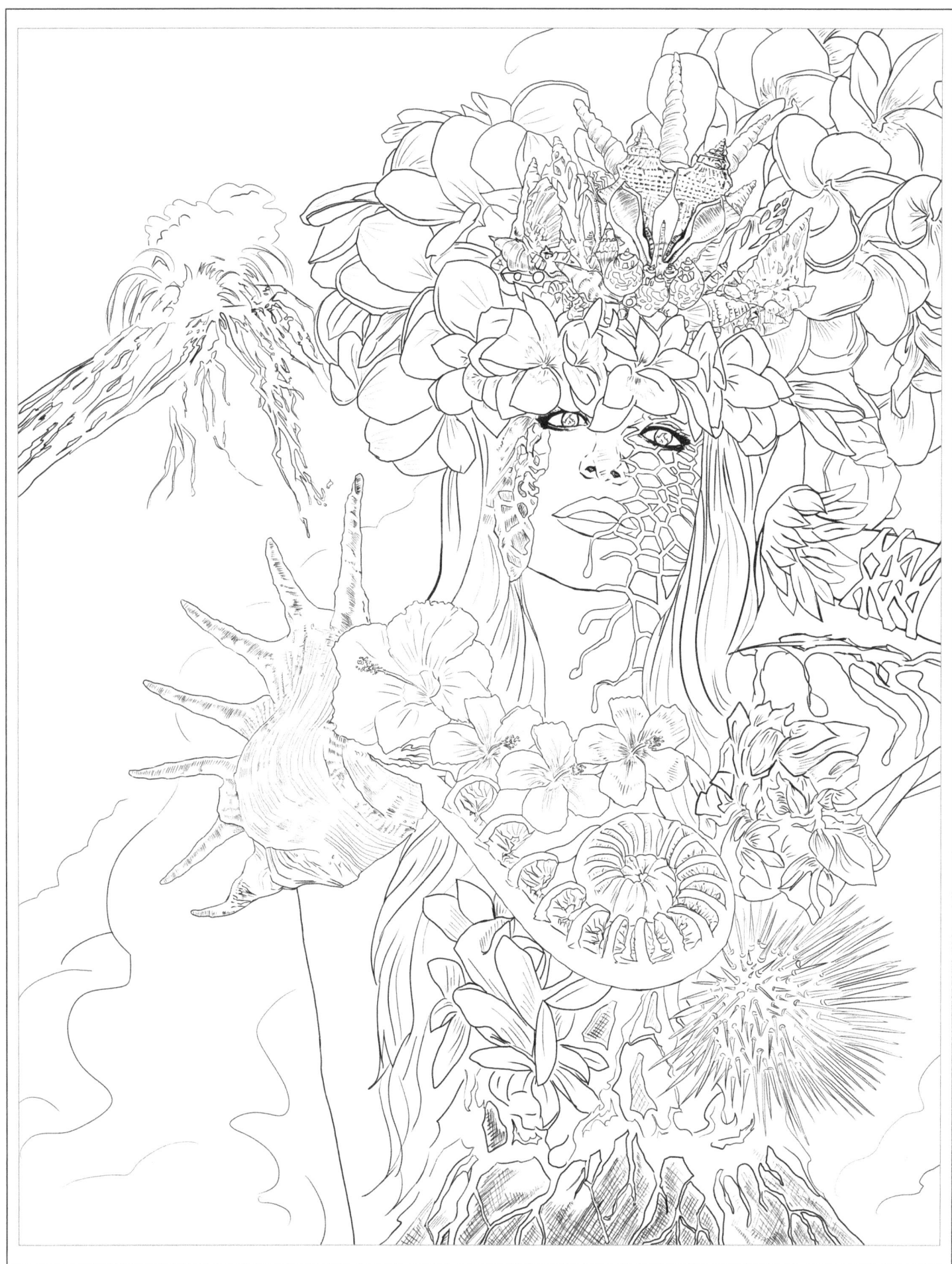

Beautiful Horror

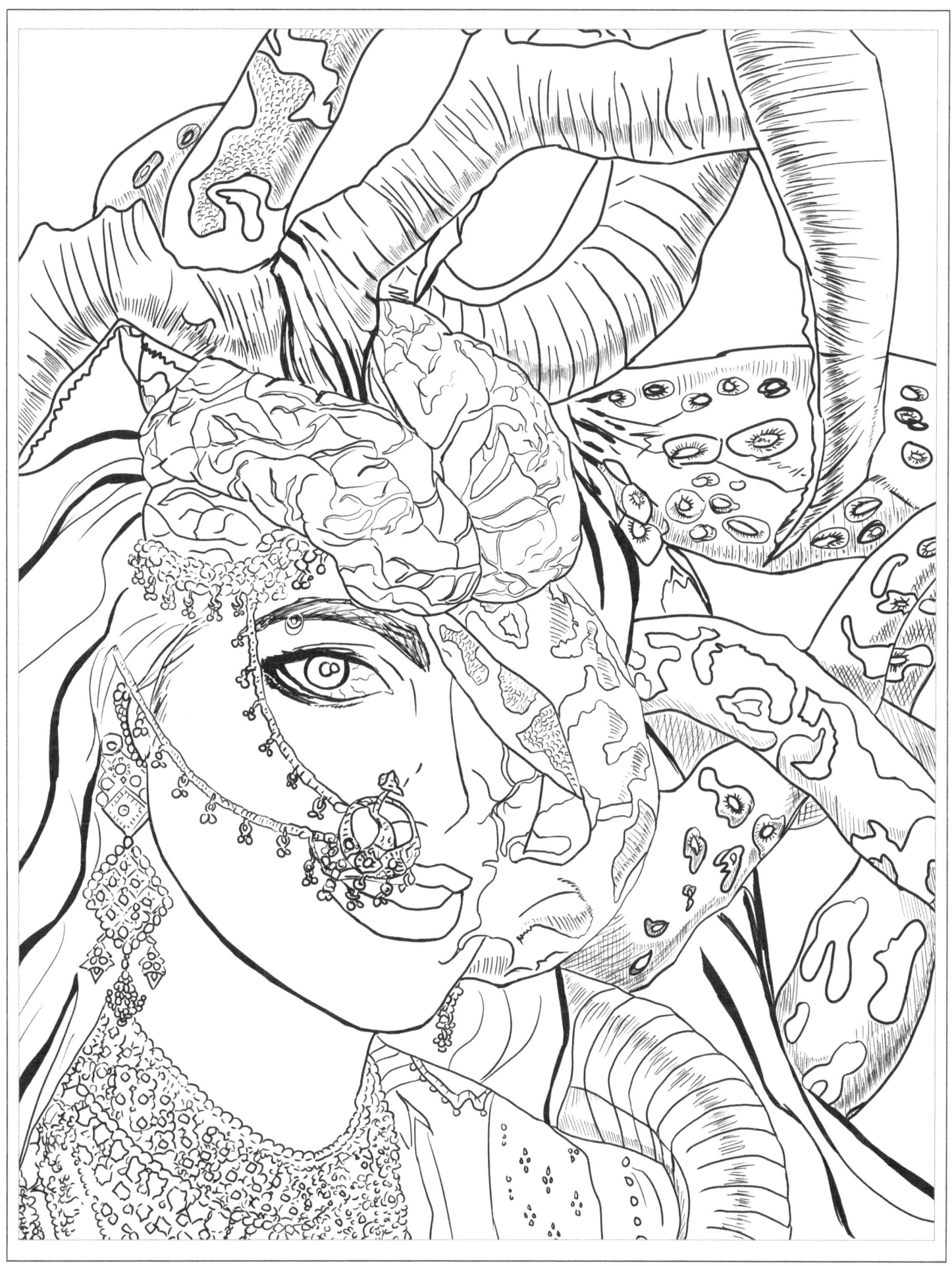

Beautiful Horror
COLORING BOOK

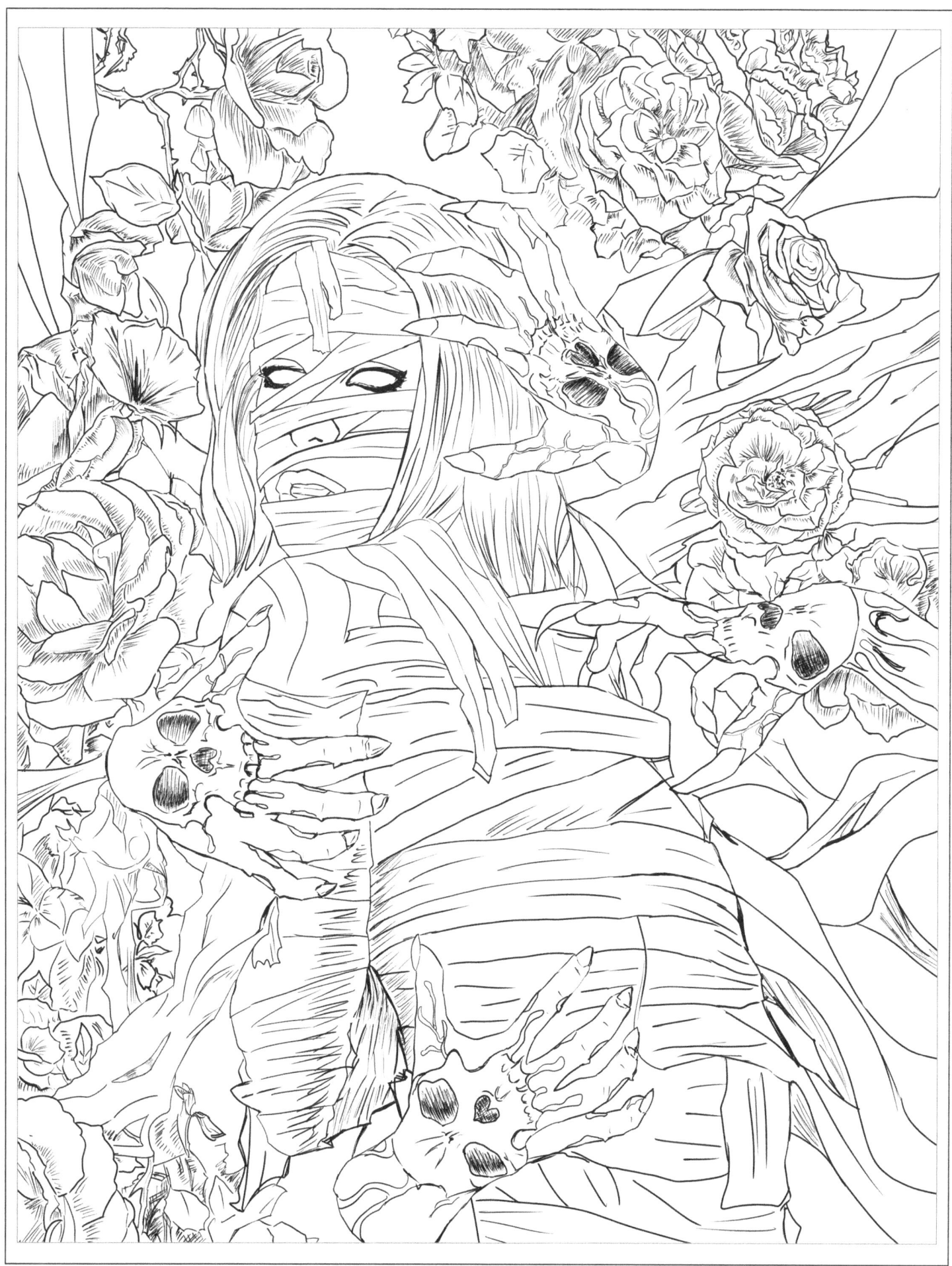

Beautiful Horror
COLORING BOOK

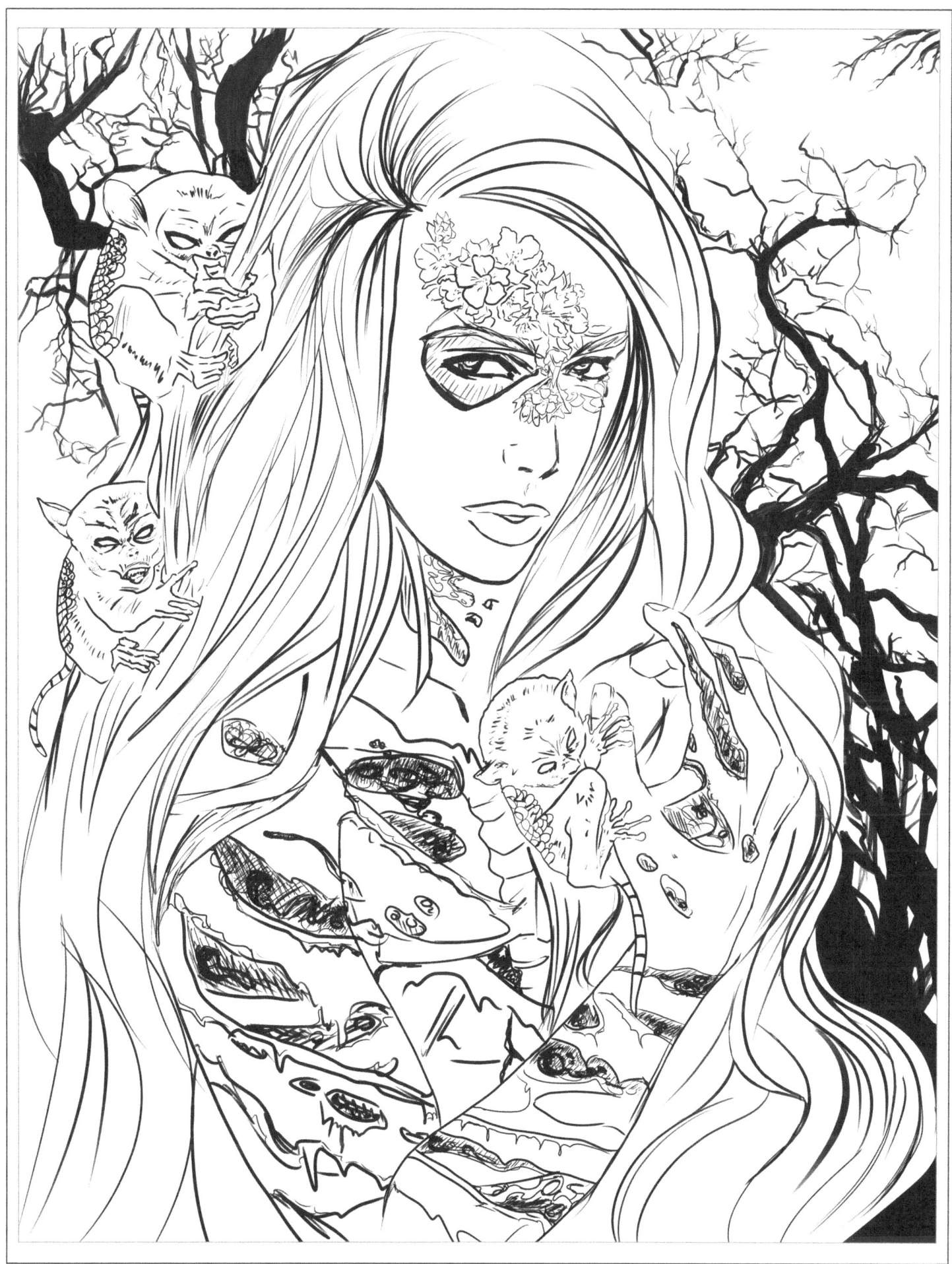

Beautiful Horror

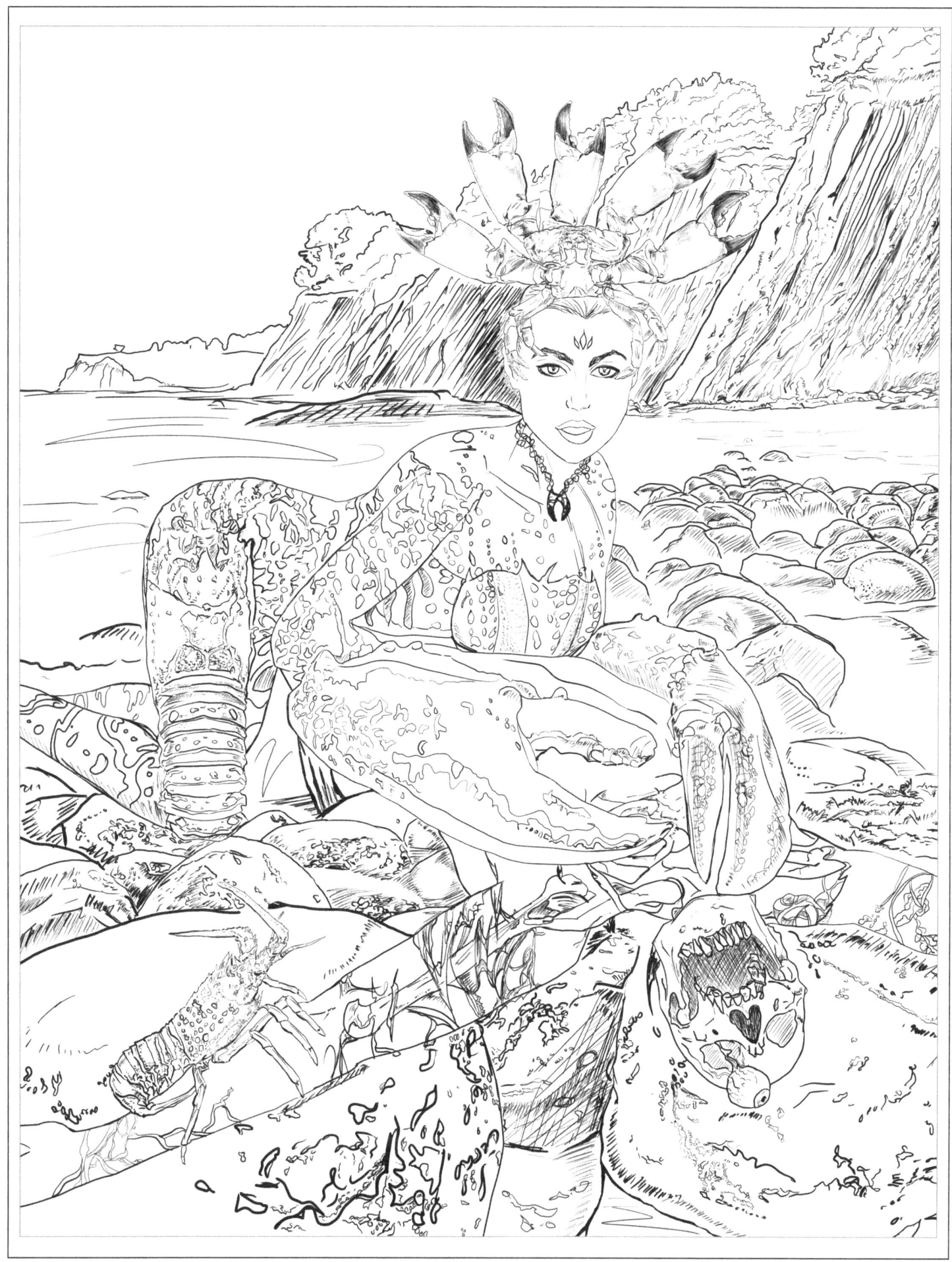

Beautiful Horror
COLORING BOOK

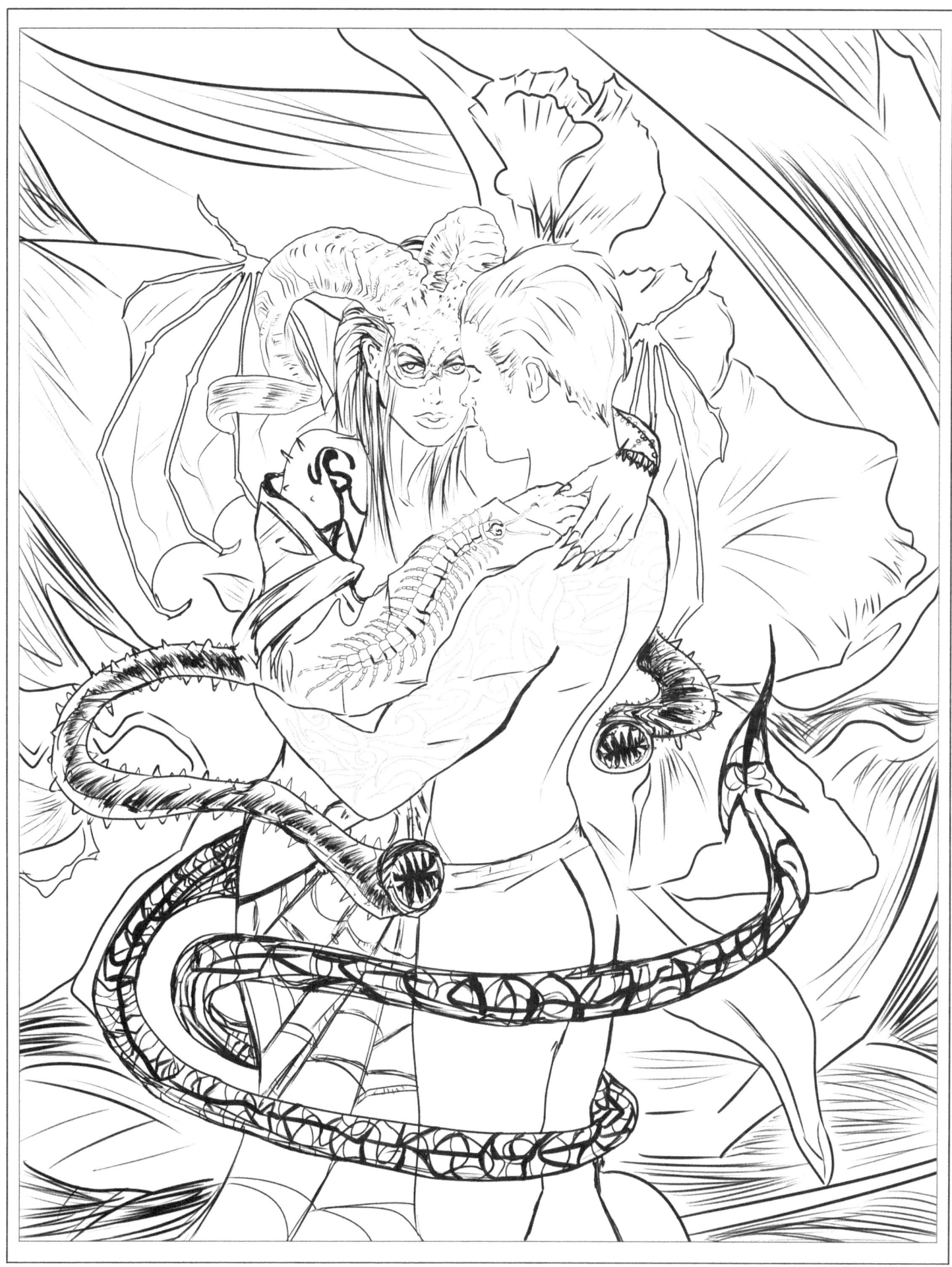

Beautiful Horror

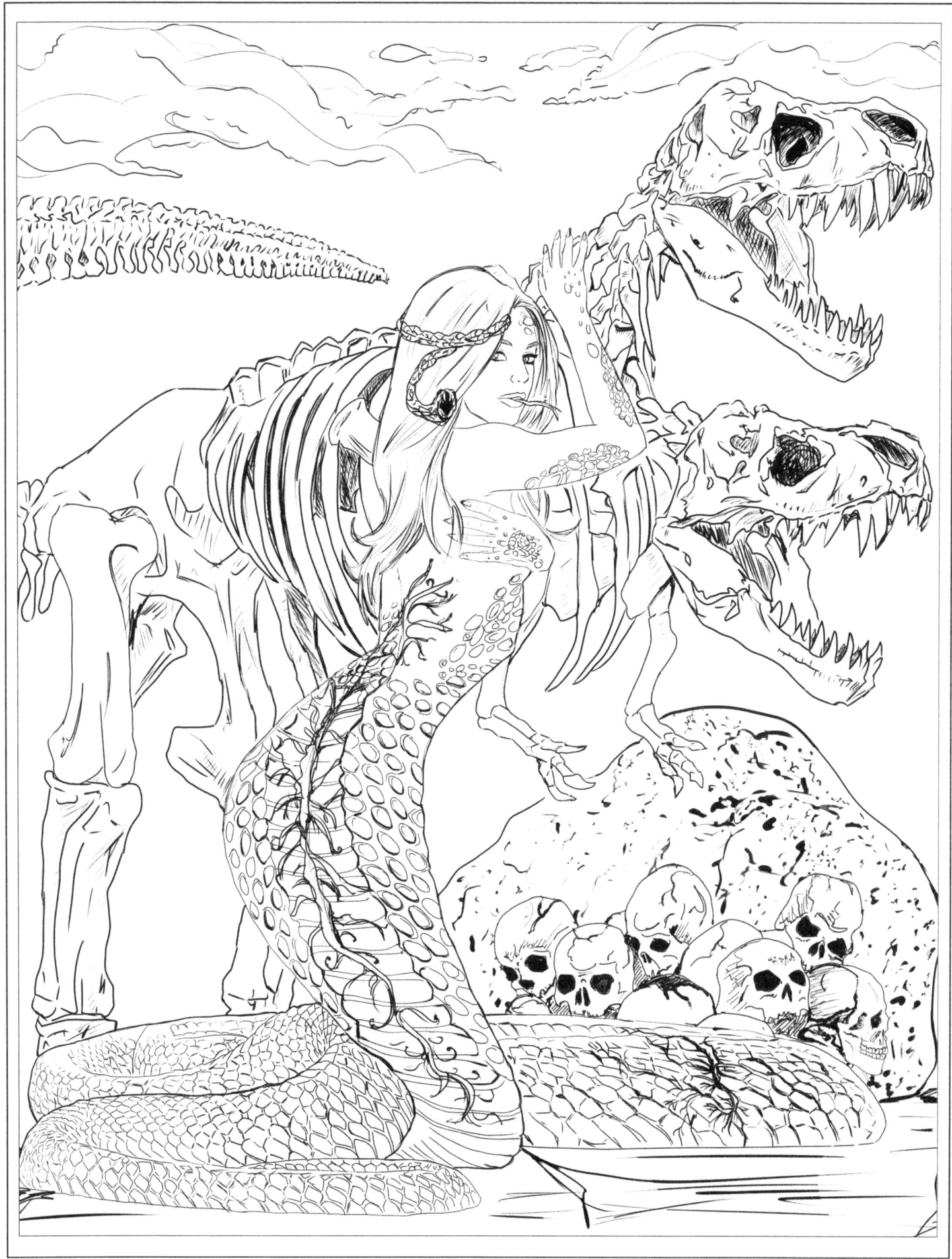

Beautiful Horror

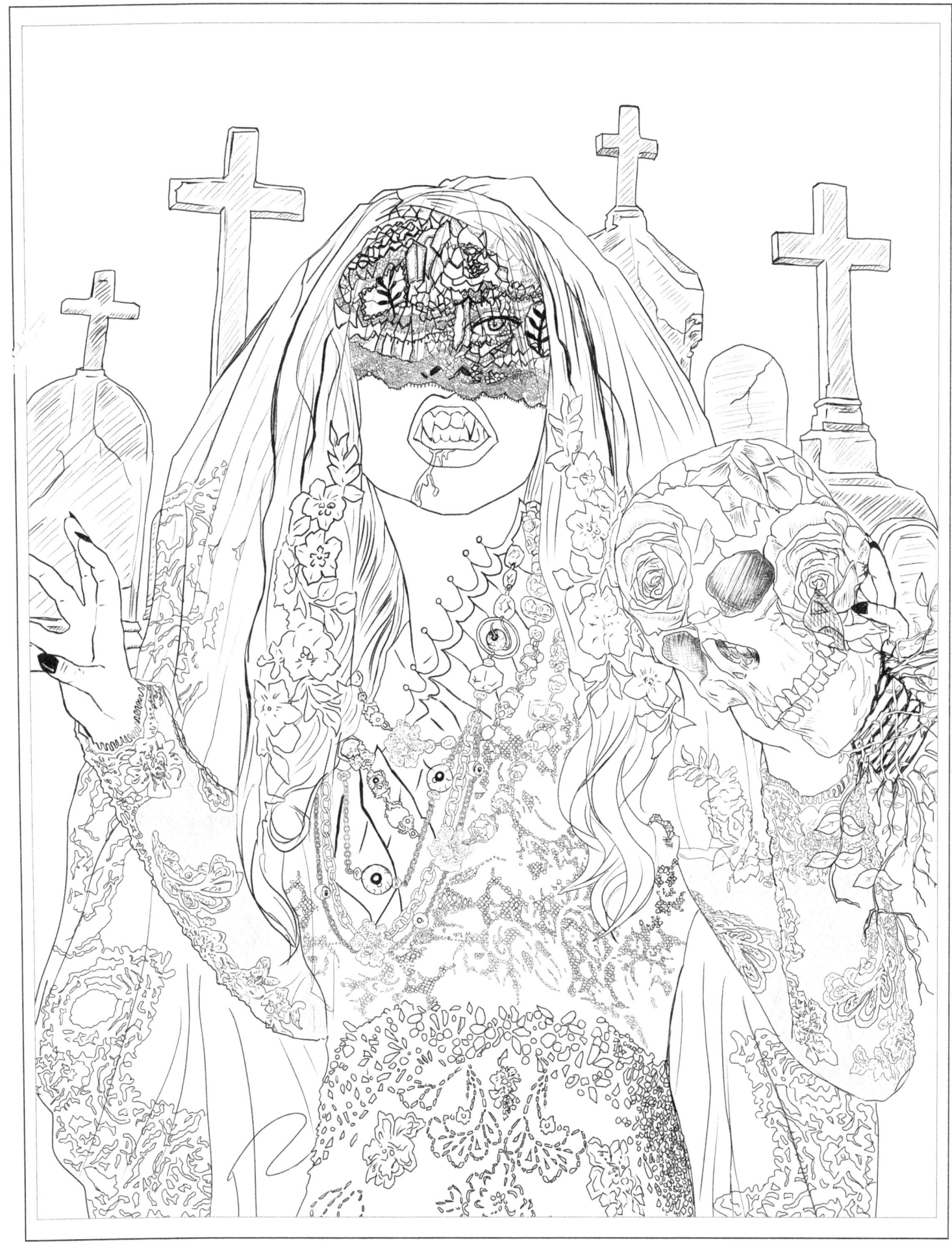

Beautiful Horror
colouring book

Also Available

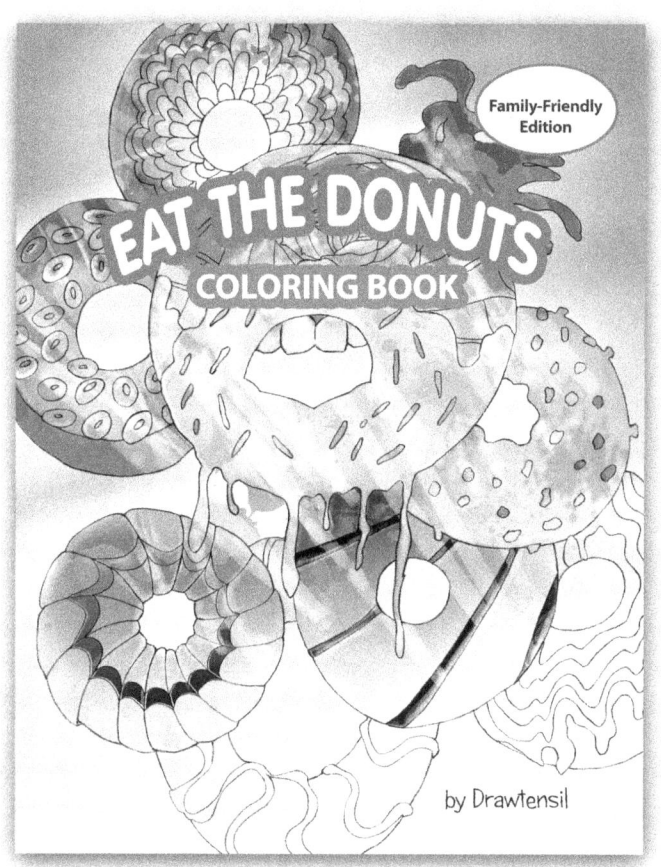
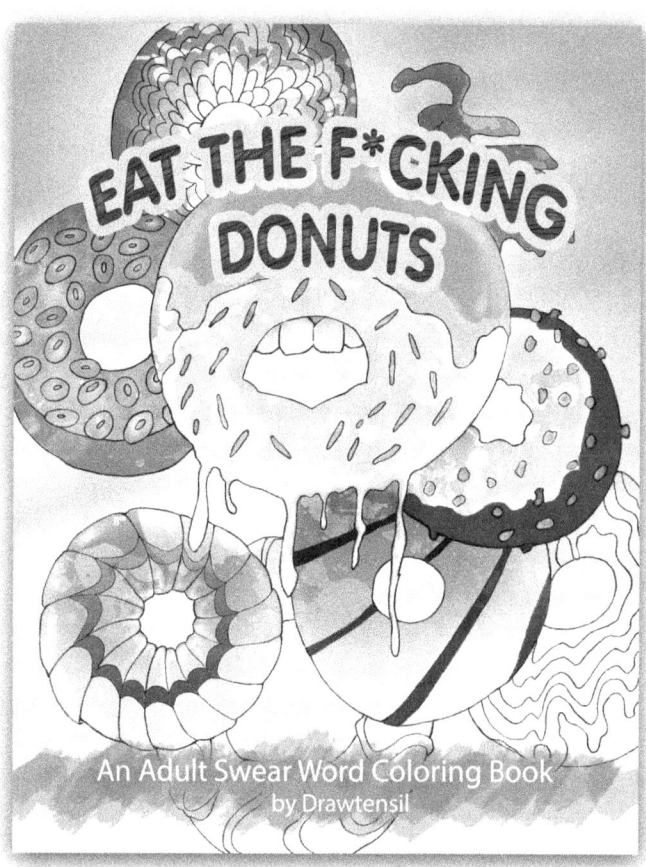

EAT THE DONUTS
Family-Friendly Edition Coloring Book

EAT THE F*CKING DONUTS
Adult Swear Word Edition Coloring Book

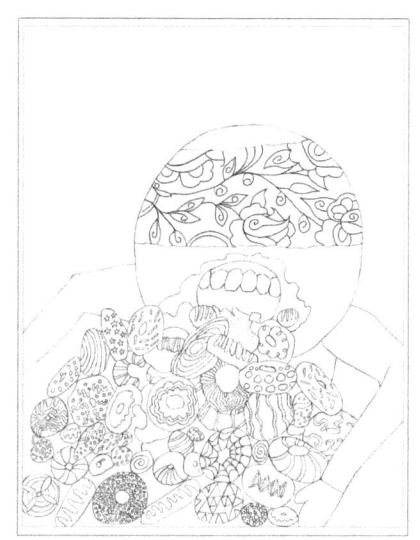
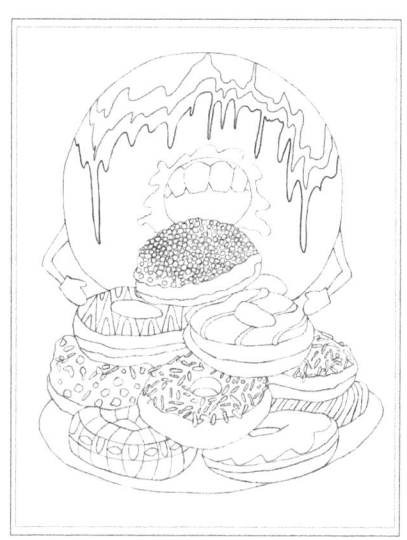
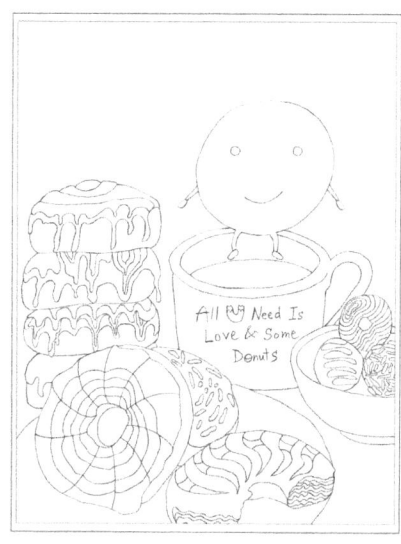

Test Your Colors Here

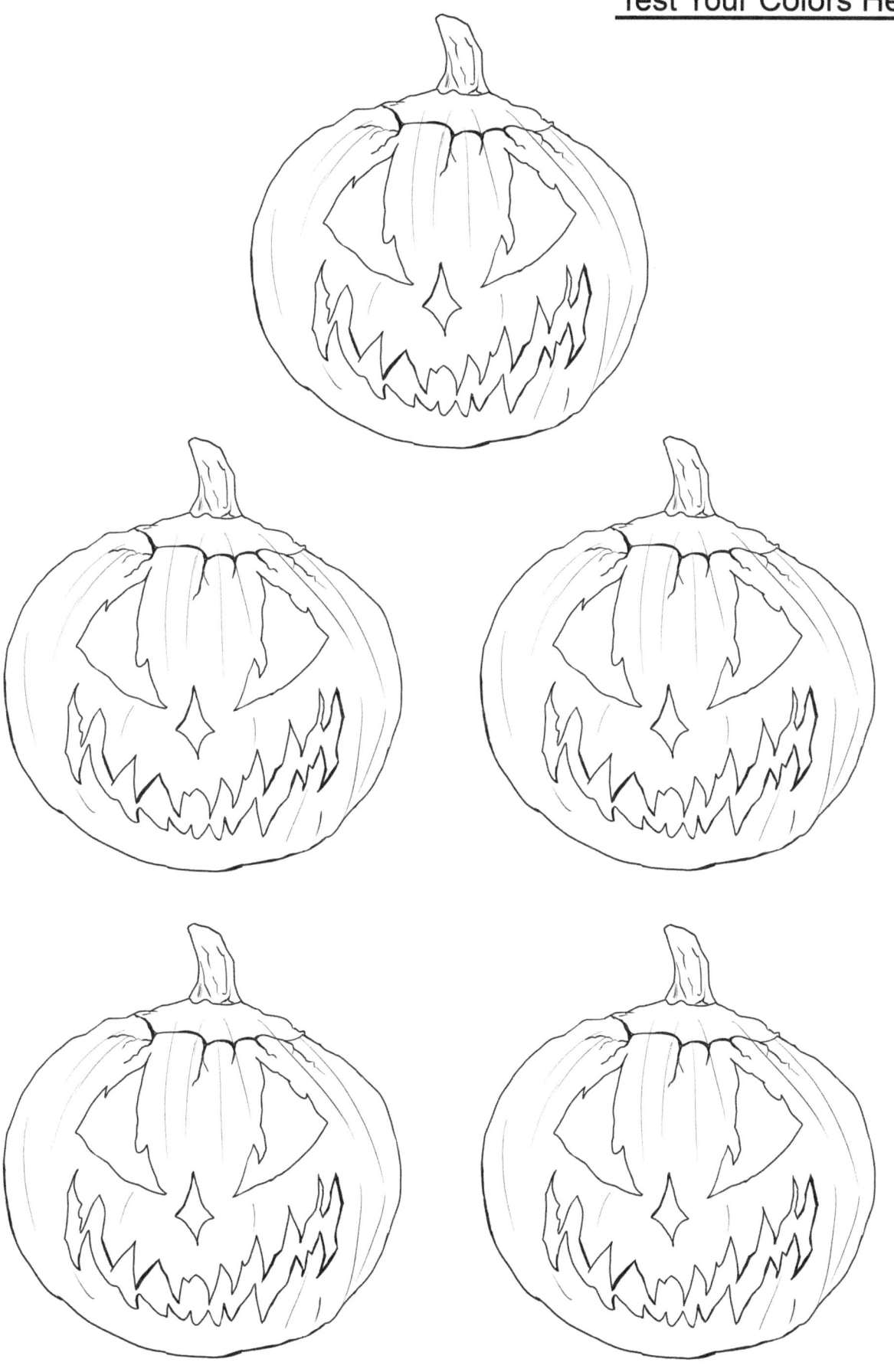

Beautiful Horror

Test Your Colors Here

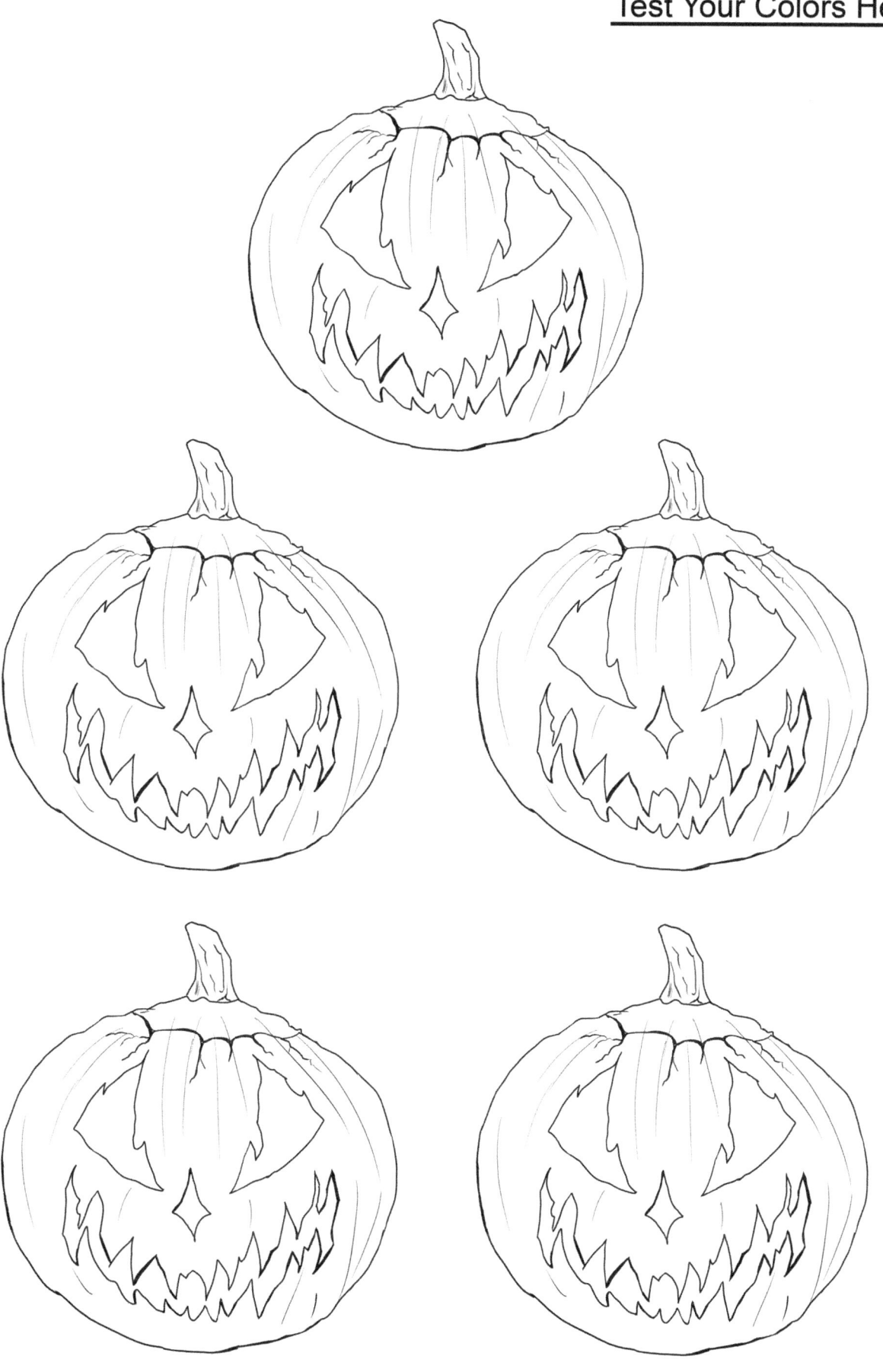

Beautiful Horror
COLORING BOOK